JULIA TUGENDHAT

Children
at the
Battle of Waterloo

Illustrated by Robin Tronson

D1492931

First published in the United Kingdom by William Heinemann in 1979 as They Were at Waterloo by Julia Dobson

Revised version Children at the Battle of Waterloo published in the United Kingdom in 2014 by Julia Tugendhat

Front Cover: by kind permission of the National Army Museum Colour oleolithograph after Richard Caton Woodville

ISBN 978-0-9570707-1-4

Produced by the Choir Press

Contents

Preface

The famous Battle of Waterloo in 1815 involved two of history's most remarkable commanders. The Emperor Napoleon Bonaparte, who led the French army was only forty-six years old at Waterloo but had fought fifty battles and won most of them. He had risen from the rank of cadet to become Consul, and then in 1804 Emperor of France. During years of war he had conquered most of Europe and replaced some of the rulers with his own allies or relatives. Then in 1812 he overreached himself by invading Russia, from where his grand army was forced into a disastrous retreat. The British, Russians, Austrians and Prussians formed a coalition and defeated the French at the Battle of Leipzig in 1813. They then invaded France, forcing Napoleon into exile on the Isle of Elba.

Wellington was also forty-six years old. His military experience had been gained in India. He had fought fewer battles than Napoleon, but with one exception, these had all been victories against superior numbers. His reputation had been made when the allied forces under his command in Spain and Portugal defeated a French army in what became known as the Peninsular War (1808–1814). Napoleon, who had never fought Wellington face to face, liked to be insulting about him. Wellington, on the other hand, acknowledged that on the battlefield Napoleon was worth 40,000 men.

The Duke of Wellington was actually at the Congress of Vienna helping to sort out the map of Europe and having a relaxed social time when the news arrived that Napoleon had escaped from Elba on the 26 February 1815 and was raising an army as he marched towards Paris. The assembled statesmen learnt, to their horror, that Napoleon was being given a rapturous welcome by his countrymen. Despite his recent defeats he was much more admired and popular than his hopeless replacement the Bourbon King Louis XVIII. Within eighteen days Napoleon had installed himself in Paris as Emperor and King Louis had fled to Belgium. The Congress agreed that Napoleon must be defeated once and for all and that the man for the job was Wellington. They appointed him Commander-in-Chief of the British and Dutch-Belgian forces assembled in Belgium. The Prussians already had an army ready under the command of Field-Marshal Prince Blücher, and Russia and Austria promised to get armies into the field as soon as possible.

1

Lord William Lennox

L ord William Lennox, the fifteen-year-old son of the Duke
of Richmond was with the Duke of Wellington at the
Congress of Vienna when Napoleon escaped from Elba. His
father, the Duke of Richmond was an old friend of Wellington
who had taken on William Lennox as an aide-de-camp.
William had joined the army as a lieutenant at the age of
thirteen. It was normal at this time for officers to buy their
way into the army. An ADC like William was treated by the
Duke as an intimate but also as a glorified messenger. He was
there to do chores for the Duke. At the same time he was
exposed to the greatest statesmen of the age, was able to
attend important meetings and social events and could learn
a great deal by watching Wellington at close hand.

When Wellington left Vienna at the end of March to take up
his command, William went with him to Brussels where he
was reunited with the rest of his family. The Duke and
Duchess of Richmond, Lord George Lennox, his older
brother and his younger sisters were comfortably installed in
a rented house in town. Many fashionable people were
staying in Brussels which was an elegant city as the army
prepared to overthrow Napoleon for the second time.

Throughout the months of April and May, Wellington and his aides were busy preparing for the impending war with the French. Money had to be raised, armaments and supplies had to be obtained, more soldiers had to be sent for and commanders had to be appointed. The various British and Dutch-Belgian regiments had to be carefully positioned in the north and west of Belgium. And close communication had to be kept with Blücher who was positioning the Prussian army in the south-east of Belgium. At this stage Wellington under-estimated Napoleon and made a big mistake. He did not think that Napoleon could possibly raise a fighting army before the month of July. He was also certain that Napoleon would cross the border from France into Belgium via Mons – a more westerly route than crossing via Charleroi in the centre. This is what he would have done had he been in Napoleon's shoes. In fact, Napoleon was at his brilliant best in the so-called 100 Days between his escape from Elba and the Battle of Waterloo. He raised and provisioned an army in record time and got the government working. He also adopted a risky but bold plan to march up the middle between Wellington's army and the Prussians, in the hope of defeating first one and then the other, thus preventing them from joining up.

In his miscalculation Wellington managed to have a good time in Brussels. He much enjoyed his social life centred around the Richmond household. There were balls, theatres, concerts and picnics, and he even took an afternoon off to take one of William's sisters to a cricket match. The Duchess of Richmond was planning a grand ball for the 15 June. It was to be the high point of the season. Just to be on the safe side she had consulted with Wellington before sending out the invitations. The Duke had assured her that all would be well. Napoleon would not be making a move yet awhile.

NAPOLEON'S MARCH

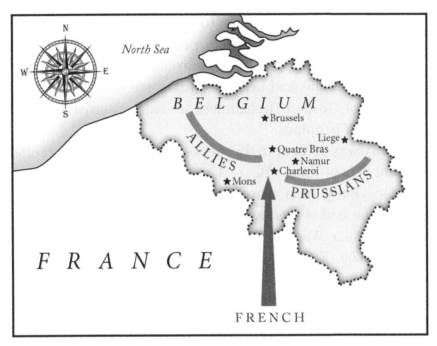

How wrong he proved to be! Napoleon actually invaded Belgium on the day of the Duchess of Richmond's ball. Wellington was caught by surprise. He had not expected Napoleon to move with such lightning speed, neither had he expected him to cross the border between the two armies at Charleroi. But things were not as bad as they looked. The French advance had been held up by a small Dutch-Belgian force at a village called Quatre Bras in the south. Meanwhile, Wellington had given the orders that set his army in motion towards Quatre Bras and he presumed that the Prussian commander, Blücher had done the same. Then, feeling quite confident enough to attend a social function, he took himself off to the ball.

3

The Duchess of Richmond was very pleased to see him because she had taken a great deal of trouble over her ball, and was relying on Wellington to make it a success. She had converted the stables and a workshop at the back of her house into a lavishly decorated ballroom. And for the general entertainment she had arranged for some sergeants of the 92nd Foot of Gordon Highlanders to dance Scottish reels to the sound of bagpipes.

Royalty was present in the person of the Prince of Orange, son and heir of King William 1 of the Netherlands. He was a likeable young man who was well known to the British because he had served as an aide-de-camp to Wellington in the Peninsular War. He had even been engaged for a short time to the English Princess Charlotte. The Duke of Brunswick was there in a black dress uniform with its silver Death's Head skull and crossbones badge. He was the ruler of a small state in Germany that had been overrun by Napoleon and had brought his own army to Belgium to help the Allies. The British commanders were more brilliant in scarlet jackets. Besides all the generals, aide-de-camps, guardsmen and cavalry officers, there were Dutch and Belgian nobility, foreign ambassadors and all the most fashionable ladies in Brussels. There were also some French notables from the court of King Louis XVIII, now in exile.

The room was abuzz with rumours and opinions. But the few officers who knew the facts about 'Boney's' invasion were not giving them away. Wellington's arrival at the ball around midnight therefore caused a flurry of attention. Here was the man who would know the answers but would any one dare to question him? He could be very haughty and cold if displeased, and one of his snubs was not easily forgotten. Lady Georgina Lennox did not fear a snub however. Wellington had dandled her on his knee when she was a little girl and she adored him. She dashed up to him and asked whether the rumours were true.

"Yes, they are true, we are off tomorrow," he replied gravely. The news was greeted with a mixture of excitement and consternation. Georgina saw the Duke of Brunswick shudder violently as if he had had a premonition of death. Officers who had ridden some distance to attend the ball hurried off to rejoin their regiments. Messengers were sent scurrying hither and thither. Quiet conversations were taking place behind the draperies. And several young ladies were clinging tearfully to their handsome partners in scarlet uniforms. They knew it was likely that the young soldiers would be killed or severely wounded on the battlefield.

Now that the waiting was over, the soldiers were eager to be off to face whatever was in store for them on the battlefield. Lord George Lennox who was William's older brother and an aide-de-camp to the Prince of Orange, went up to his bedroom to prepare for departure. William sadly watched him go. He should have been packing too, but had fallen off his horse a week earlier and had broken an arm and damaged an eye. Wellington would not hear of him going to fight with a bandaged head and an arm in a sling. William tried not to show his disappointment and continued to circulate among the guests, as if nothing out of the ordinary was happening. He saw Wellington chatting to his sister Georgina in the supper room as if he had not a care in the world. It was only when the Commander-in-Chief took his leave at the front door that he showed he had graver matters on his mind. He asked the Duke of Richmond whether there was a good map in the house. Richmond took him into his study and spread one out before him. "Napoleon has humbugged me, by God!"

Wellington announced. "He has gained twenty-four hours march on me. I have ordered the army to concentrate at Quatre Bras, but we shall not stop him there, and if so I must fight him here." He jabbed with his thumb at a spot just south of the village of Waterloo.

Napoleon now had the advantage of surprise and the chance to deal with the Prussians before the Allied army got to the spot. He also had an army of which he could be proud. Many of his commanders had returned to serve him, men of zeal and ability who had risen to the top through merit and not through birth or the purchase of commissions. There was the red-headed Marshal Ney, whose amazing courage in the Russian retreat had earned him the title of the 'bravest of the brave.' When Napoleon was a prisoner on the Isle of Elba he had joined the royalists. Hearing the news of his escape Ney had sworn that he would bring Napoleon back in chains. But when he met his charismatic commander again he abandoned the Bourbons and offered his services to Napoleon. There were the Marshals Soult and Grouchy, who also had sworn loyalty to Louis XVIII but who could not resist the call of their old leader. The corps commanders included men like d'Erlon, Reille, and Vandamme who had years of military experience behind them.

In the ranks were many veterans, seasoned soldiers who had helped Napoleon win so many victories in the past. Courage and ability in the ranks were rewarded and the men were ready to lay down their lives once more for their beloved Emperor. Then there was Napoleon himself, who seemed to have lost nothing of his magic hold over his troops. He had led them to victory time and again and was expected to do so again. They were united in his cause. The British army opposing him had too many 'Johnny Newcomes' among them, but the veterans had shown themselves capable of beating the French in the Peninsular War. Of the Allied units, the King's German Legion was considered equal to the British. The KGL, as it was commonly called, had been formed by Hanoverian soldiers who had escaped to England after their country's army had been conquered by Napoleon in 1803. Starting with one weak regiment, the KGL had built itself into a strong, well-trained body that included cavalry (horse soldiers), infantry (foot soldiers) and artillery (gunners). The other German force gathered together by the Duke of Brunswick contained more inexperienced youth than any other formation but the 'Black Duke' was considered to be a man of courage.

The Dutch-Belgians were rather more suspect. It was common knowledge that many of the officers and men would rather have been fighting, as they had recently done, on the side of Napoleon. The loyalty of their commander, the Prince of Orange, was not in doubt, but he had been given the command of the 1st corps because of his royal status and at twenty-two was too young for such a position of responsibility.

However, if there was one man capable of holding together this motley army it was Wellington. 'Nosey' was not adored by his troops as was Napoleon but they trusted him completely and would do what was needed of them. Neither did he have Napoleon's showy military brilliance, but as a master of defensive tactics there was no one to equal him.

Lord Uxbridge, a dashing cavalry officer, had been appointed the Second-in-Command by the Duke of York against Wellington's wishes. But his appointment was popular with the army as a whole. So was the choice of Lord Hill as a corps commander. He was a reliable, experienced soldier who had fought under Wellington in the Peninsula. He had a ruddy cheerful face and was adored by the soldiers who looked up to him as a father. Divisional commanders included men like Cooke, Alten, Perponcher and Picton with sound military reputations. The Quartermaster-General was a brilliant young man called Sir William de Lancey. An American by birth he had joined the British army at the age of eleven.

Wellington's Prussian allies were not noted for their efficiency, but at least they did not suffer from divided loyalties. Although Field Marshal Blücher was seventy-two he was still an enthusiastic man of action. He looked his age with his bushy white moustache, lined face and receding hair but he was still the hard-riding, hard-drinking swearing hussar of his youth. He had a way of coming back after defeat that had earned him the nickname of 'Forwards.' He was a loyal, brave, old-fashioned soldier who was adored by his troops. What he lacked in intellect was made up for by his very clever Chief-of-Staff Gneisenau who hated Napoleon and wanted to defeat him. Baron von Müffling, the Prussian representative on Wellington's staff, was also a man to be trusted. If the Allies and the Prussians could act together, their chances of defeating Napoleon would be so much greater. Wellington certainly thought so.

Brussels was a small place and everyone knew of the conversation that the writer and Radical Member of Parliament Mr Thomas Creevey had had with Wellington some weeks earlier. When Creevey had asked the Duke what he would make of the coming battle, Wellington had replied, "By God! I think Blücher and myself can do the thing. There," he said, pointing to a British infantryman who had come into sight, "there, it all depends upon that article whether we do the business or not. Give me enough of it, and I am sure."

2

Mary Adwicke

By the early hours of Friday 16 June many of the infantry-men in whom Wellington reposed so much faith were on their way to Quatre Bras. They were marching steadily away from Brussels down the paved road called a chaussée accompanied by officers mounted on horses. Wagons and supply carts were squeezed into the intervals between the regiments, and women and children were straggling alongside.

Among them was a six-year-old girl called Mary Adwicke. She was trying to keep up with her mother, who in turn was trying to keep up with her father who was marching to war with his regiment. Mary Adwicke was a camp follower and had been since the day she was born. Her Irish mother was married to John Adwicke who was a sergeant in Captain Crowe's Company in the 32nd Regiment of Foot. A small proportion of wives were allowed to attach themselves to companies. They were not paid but were allowed half rations in exchange for washing, cooking and mending for their husbands and fellow soldiers. Their children were on quarter rations. Where John Adwicke went, Mary and her mother followed. They had trailed after the army through Spain, Portugal and France. More recently, while the 32nd had been stationed in Brussels, they had stayed in lodgings on the outskirts of the town. When Napoleon invaded Belgium they had had to leave their comfortable lodgings at very short notice. They were used to sudden moves, but this time it had been a wrench. Mrs Adwicke had recently had a baby and had been glad to have a roof over her head. But she had chosen the life and was hardened to it, so she packed up their few possessions, wrapped baby John in a shawl and set off briskly for war.

It was twenty-one miles from Brussels to Quatre Bras and the women and children were relieved when the soldiers called a halt in the forest of Soignes near the village of Waterloo to have their breakfast. While they were resting, the Duke of Wellington and his staff rode by. The Duke was instantly recognizable amongst his glittering entourage by his simple appearance. Lean and wiry, he had short brown hair, blue eyes and a prominent straight nose. He wore a dark blue frock coat and a matching cloak. His well-known black hat was worn with the points facing to the front and back. On it was the black cockade of King George and three others in the colours of Spain, Portugal and the Netherlands in which he held the rank of Field-Marshal. He was mounted on his eight-year-old chestnut charger Copenhagen. Copenhagen was a kicker and mounted officers were careful to keep their distance. But he was immensely strong and had already been back and forth from Quatre Bras. The Duke did not like his soldiers to cheer him, but they stood up respectfully as he passed. John Adwicke lifted Mary up so that she could see the great man who sat so erect and neat on his horse.

The march was not resumed until after midday. It was then that a messenger galloped up on horseback with orders for the soldiers to leave their heavy baggage behind and to make all possible speed towards Quatre Bras. When the bugle sounded the men to their feet an officer was clearly heard to say, "There goes my death warrant." Even though it was an extremely hot summer day the soldiers set off at such a fast pace the women and children were left far behind.

It was fortunate that most of them had been toughened up during the Peninsular campaigns, for the journey was grueling and they carried very heavy rifles and all their kit. As they marched along they could hear the crashing boom of guns and could see rising plumes of thick black smoke. This fog swallowed up the soldiers in blue or black uniforms. Only the scarlet infantry coats showed up in the smoke. The heat was intense and they passed several soldiers dead of heat-stroke by the roadside. In one village barrels of water had been left out for the soldiers and the women and children were grateful to be able to drink from them in their turn.

By questioning the wounded, the women gradually pieced together the day's events. They discovered that there were in fact two battles in progress. The Prussians, led by Blücher were fighting part of the French army under Napoleon at a place called Ligny, further to the east, while the Allies were in combat with the rest of the French army under the command of Marshal Ney at the crossroads of Quatre Bras. Wellington was in the risky position of being outnumbered since many of his troops, including the cavalry, had not yet reached the spot.

When the camp followers reached the edge of the battle Mary and her mother searched for John Adwicke among the thousand or so wounded who had been laid up in the farm-houses. Happily they did not find him but were distressed to see how many soldiers of the 32nd had been badly hurt, although they had been fighting for less than two hours. The

BATTLES OF QUATRE BRAS & LIGNY - 16 JUNE 1815

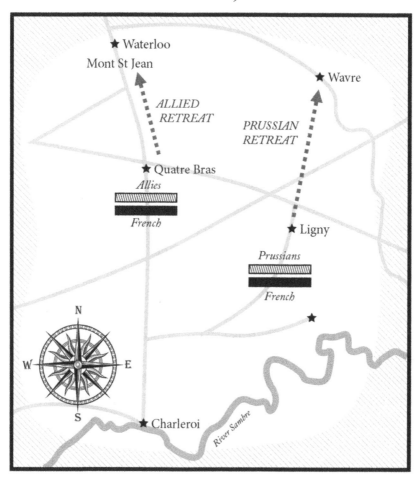

92nd Highlanders (some of whom had danced at the Duchess of Richmond's ball) had also suffered dreadfully, as had the Brunswickers, who had lost their commander. The Duke of Brunswick's premonition of death had come true. He had been hit by a musket ball in the stomach while trying to rally his countrymen after a French attack. His body was carried off the battlefield by his faithful soldiers in in their black uniforms.

The battle was not going well for the Allies and those in the rear were tempted to flee. Some of them took off when some French cavalrymen overshot their own lines and ended up in the courtyard of the farmhouse where the Adwickes were sheltering. But Mrs Adwicke and Mary stayed put and in due course their patience was rewarded when the Foot Guards, the most famous of British infantrymen, reached Quatre Bras. They marched straight into the wood to clear out the French. At six-thirty in the evening a familiar bugle note was heard. It was the signal to advance. Even Mary knew that Wellington never advanced unless victory was in his grasp. By nine o'clock the French had been chased from the field and the battle of Quatre Bras was over.

The black cloud of cannon smoke gradually lifted and the sounds of battle died down. There was silence too in the direction of Ligny, where Blücher had been fighting the French, though no one knew what had been the outcome of that struggle. The women, who had kept together all day, now separated in search of their husbands, whom they were as likely to find dead as alive. Still clutching the baby, and holding Mary by the hand, Mrs Adwicke set out on the last grim mission of the day.

The carnage was terrible. Thousands of dead and dying men and horses were strewn across the field. The air was filled with the moans and groans of men who cried out for water and the unearthly sound of horses in agony. The lucky ones were carried off the field by members of their companies but the rest were at the mercy of the looters (soldiers included) who crept out in the darkness and removed clothes, shoes, food, coins and even teeth from both the living and dead. Some even stabbed the wounded to death. The survivors, by now insensitive to the noise and the stench were camping down among the corpses. Mother and daughter picked their way through the grizzly remains of battle until they came upon the 32nd where they had a joyful reunion with John Adwicke, who was alive and well. Three men had been killed and many wounded in his company so he considered himself lucky to be alive.

The Adwickes withdrew a little way from the main camp and built a fire of their own. The trees in the wood had been so badly damaged in the fighting that firewood was to be had for the taking. They put a skinny chicken in the camp kettle to boil. Mary was a skilled scavenger and had caught it near the farmhouse during the afternoon. After they had eaten, they stretched out together on the bloodstained ground and went to sleep, untroubled by the sounds of suffering around them.

Saturday 17 June dawned fair. While Mrs Adwicke fed the baby, Mary boiled the kettle, and John set about cleaning his equipment. The general opinion was that the battle would be resumed that day, and everyone was preparing accordingly. Detachments from the various regiments were busy burying their dead and bringing in their wounded. But when the orders came it was for a silent and speedy retreat. This surprised them but then they did not have the same information as Wellington. They did not know that the Prussians had been beaten, though not destroyed by Napoleon at Ligny. Neither did they know that the Prussian army, pursued by a French force under Marshal Grouchy, had fallen back in a north-easterly direction on Wavre, thus making it necessary for Wellington to fall back also, for he could not afford to be caught between Ney and Napoleon.

It was the camp followers and the wounded who generally had the worst time in a retreat. This occasion was no exception. Mother and daughter tried to keep up with the 32nd but did not have the strength. When they stumbled and fell John Adwicke was not allowed to fall out of line to help them. The wounded dropped back so far that some of them were captured and taken behind French lines. Fortunately, the British cavalry, who had missed the battle, arrived in time to guard the retreating army from the French with whom they had some sharp skirmishes.

The hardships of the stragglers were made worse by the weather. In the morning it was hot and sticky. In the afternoon a violent thunderstorm broke out. Rain came pouring down in torrents and soon the fields were a quagmire of mud and horse dung. Mary and her mother somehow managed to keep going. They were very sorry for poor Mrs Deacon who was struggling along beside them. She was expecting a baby any day, and had three others in tow. She was frantically looking for her husband who had been wounded at Quatre Bras.

They wearily retraced their footsteps, passing on the way the inns of Le Caillou and La Belle Alliance until they came up with the army which was settling down for the night at the crossroads on a ridge called Mont St Jean just south of the village of Waterloo, the very spot where Wellington had predicted he might have to fight. They said goodbye to Mrs Deacon who, though heavily pregnant, was determined to walk fifteen more miles to Brussels in the hope of finding her husband. They themselves were fortunate enough to find John Adwicke without difficulty because the 32nd was making camp close to the main road.

All night long the rain bucketed down accompanied by

lightening and thunder. For those camping out in the open it was too wet to build fires so many soldiers went without food. All through the wretched night they heard the sounds of weapons, hooves and cartwheels as the French came into position on the other side of the valley. Despite the discomfort John Adwicke was in a cheerful mood for he believed that the storm was a good omen. All Wellington's greatest victories in the Peninsula had been preceded by a storm. It was lucky weather – 'Wellington weather.' Anyway Wellington himself was famous for being lucky. Throughout all the tough battles in Spain and Portugal he had had some close calls but had avoided being captured or wounded.

3

William Leeke

Among the soldiers who bestirred themselves on the ridge in the cold drizzly dawn of Sunday 18 June was an officer of seventeen called William Leeke. He had only been in the army for five weeks and was about to face his first battle. He came from a naval family, but after his oldest brother had been killed in action his mother had been opposed to his joining the navy. She had not wanted him to join the army either and had pressed him to enter the church. But Leeke had had his own ideas and bought himself a commission and uniform as an ensign in the 52nd Light Infantry whose commander was his cousin, Sir John Colborne.

The night before the battle was the first night he had spent in the open with his regiment. He spent it jumping up and down to avoid being trampled on by some horses that were galloping around in terror of the storm. When dawn broke he felt so exhausted he hardly knew what to do with himself. He saw a camp fire not far off, and without considering whether he was doing the right thing or not, he made his way towards it. It belonged to the company of another regiment who were kind enough to make him welcome. Taking full advantage of their kindness, Leeke stretched himself out on a plank near the fire and slept soundly for three hours. He might have slept longer had not a soldier from his own company come over to tell him that breakfast was ready.

Leeke tried to smarten himself up. First of all he removed his boat cloak that had given him some protection from the torrential rain. He was immensely proud of this cloak he had bought in London. He had gladly lent the detachable hood and cape to Sir John Colborne who was in need of waterproof covering. He smoothed down his red jacket, put on his shako that looked like a tall black top hat with peak and plume and tested the sword in its scabbard to make sure that it had not rusted. Then he eagerly presented himself for breakfast, which consisted of a dry biscuit and some soup heated up in a mess tin. Leeke ate his biscuit while the soup was being passed from hand to hand. When it came to his turn he raised the tin to his lips, but before he had a chance to swallow a fellow officer said, "Master Leeke, I think you have had your share of that."

Leeke was mortified and quickly passed on the tin untouched. But he felt so much better after his rest that he did not remain downhearted for long. His natural curiosity soon got the better of him and he began to look around. The Allied army was spread out on the ridge of Mont St Jean along a front about three miles long. A partly sunken road ran along the crest of the ridge from west to east. This sunken road was bisected by the main Brussels to Charleroi road. These cross-roads marked the centre of the Allied line. To the east was the left wing of the army and to the west was the right wing.

Leeke's own regiment, the 52nd Light Infantry, was far over on the right wing. Though he had never been in a battle he could see that the defensive position Wellington had chosen was a good one. The road, which had hedges, was a natural obstacle, while the ridge and slope behind it offered good cover. The fields in the valley were planted with clover and rye that grew much taller than the varieties we have today, thus offering further concealment. The line was strengthened by three groups of buildings. To the east were the farm buildings of Papelotte and Frichermont. To the west was the village of Braine L'Alleud. The farmhouses of Hougoumont and La Haye Sainte were focal points in the centre of the line.

Wellington decided to leave Hougoumont in the hands of the British Foot Guards who were the pick of his troops, under the command of Colonel James Macdonnell. They were to be supported by Dutch Nassauers who had played a crucial role in holding the French at bay at Quatre Bras. Macdonnell was a commander in whom Wellington had perfect trust. He chose the green-jacketed 2nd Light Battalion, of the KGL under Major George Baring to defend La Haye Sainte. Baring was an experienced officer who had served in the Peninsula.

On the 18 June Wellington had 73,200 men and 157 guns at Waterloo plus another 17,000 men and 22 guns further away near Hal. The various regiments had been moving into place since dawn. Skirmishers were finding concealed positions right out in front of the line. These men formed a buffer between the main army and the enemy. They were sharpshooters, acted as individuals and their task was to intercept attacks and to harass the enemy. The infantry had formed up on the slope behind the ridge. Wellington had wisely interspersed his trusted British regiments with weaker inexperienced Allied troops. The cavalry spaced out behind them. The heavy cavalry had been positioned right in the middle of the line on either side of the crossroads, while a number of Dutch-Belgian and German troops had been put further back still as a reserve.

Field guns were drawn up at intervals along the line in front of the ridge. Artillery would play an important part in the battle, and Wellington had given careful thought to the placing of his guns which consisted of nine and six-pounder cannon and howitzers Some of the field guns were in fixed positions and would not be moved again that day. Others, in the hands of the Royal Horse Artillery, were mobile. Leeke had heard a great deal about this branch of the army with its professionally trained officers who did not buy their commissions. He had to admit that they looked very fine as they brought their guns up at a gallop. The gunners in their smart blue uniforms could unlimber or unhitch the guns from the horses, and limber them up again in a matter of minutes.

The cannon and howitzers fired a variety of missiles: round shot, common shell, canister, and spherical case. A round shot was made of solid iron and either weighed six or nine pounds. It had an effective range of 600-700 metres. It was a fearsome killer of men and horses. It could plough through twenty men in a row like a cheese slicer. Not much remained of a body that was in the way of round shot. A shell was made of a cast-iron covering filled with gunpowder and equipped with a fuse. When the gunpowder exploded, the shell case burst in all directions. A canister or case was a cylindrical container of thin metal that was filled with musket balls, pellets or scrap. The heavy canister was sometimes called grape. A spherical case (invented some years earlier by Henry Shrapnel of the Royal Artillery) contained numerous musket balls that burst out of the case when the gunpowder charge went off. Howitzers were a type of cannon that could fire missiles up at a high angle. They had short barrels so did not fire round shot. Their role was to lob shells at the enemy and the exploding shells they fired could be deadly against troops in the open or behind cover. Another weapon on the battlefield was the rocket, beloved by its inventor Sir William Congreve but disliked by Wellington and still so inaccurate it was considered something of a joke.

Across the valley on the opposite ridge Leeke could see and hear signs of activity. The French deployed 77,500 men and 246 guns, with another 30,00 men and 96 guns away to the east under Grouchy. Not only did the French outnumber the Allied army but they had heavier guns. Leeke had heard horrible tales of the twelve-pounders that Napoleon called his 'most beautiful daughters.' As the French troops assembled they looked magnificent. Leeke could clearly see the shiny metal breastplates of the famous Cuirassiers, the bright pennants of the Lancers, and the brass helmets of the Dragoons who were bringing their horses up behind the ranks of dark blue-coated infantrymen. When he heard martial music and frenzied shouts of "Vive l'Empereur" Leeke knew that Napoleon was reviewing his troops in person, and he could not help feeling nervous in the face of these awesome preparations.

He looked down at the peaceful valley between the two sides. The sun had come out and the crops were drying out. The two armies were only three-quarters of a mile apart, and Leeke found it hard to imagine how the two large armies would be able to move about in such a small space. The French seemed in no hurry to start the attack. The hours slipped by and nothing happened. It was a trying time for veteran and new recruit alike and Leeke found himself wishing that the battle would start.

He felt more cheerful when Lord Hill rode past at ten o'clock. The corps commander beamed at his troops and Leeke felt sure that a special smile had been bestowed on

BATTLE OF WATERLOO JUNE 18

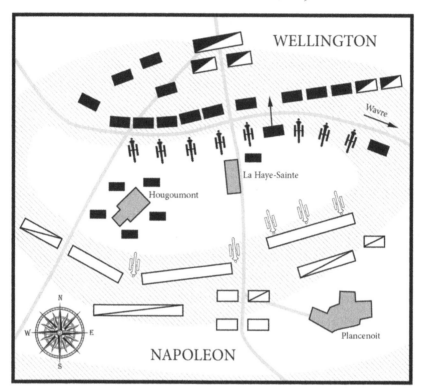

WELLINGTON

Wavre

La Haye-Sainte

Hougoumont

Plancenoit

N

W — E

S

NAPOLEON

KEY: *Infantry   Cavalry   Artillery*

him. Shortly afterwards, the regiment was called to arms, and Leeke was told that he and another young ensign called Nettles were to carry the colours that day. As the youngest ensign in his regiment he was given the task of carrying the regimental flag while Nettles was to carry the Union Jack. The colours at this time were enormous, six feet square, and requiring considerable physical strength to handle. If either flag fell into enemy hands, the 52nd would feel disgraced. The fate of the flags was not left only in the hands of novices however. Leeke and Nettles were each assigned an experienced senior sergeant to look after them. After an initial attack of nerves Leeke felt pleased and proud to have been chosen.

But he was not at all happy when he was ordered to the right wing of the regiment. He wanted to stay in the left wing with the officers he had got to know in the short time he had been in the army. He was so upset at being separated from his friends that he even dared to suggest that the proper place for the regimental colour he was carrying was on the left wing. The officer, who had more pressing matters on his mind, paid him no attention, and Leeke was forced to take the position he had been given. In any event, there was no time for brooding. At eleven-thirty, the first shot was fired from a French cannon. More shots followed, some of which even reached the high ground well behind the lines where the 52nd was standing in reserve. Rhodes, the colour sergeant pointed one out. "There Mr Leeke, is a cannon shot, if you never saw one before."

4

The French Drummer Boy

———⁘———

On the other side of the valley from Leeke, a young drummer boy was also waiting for the action to start. Many young boys were employed on both sides as drummers. Their task was to beat out a rhythm on their drums to which the infantry could march. Sometimes, officers instructed them to beat out commands when orders by mouth could not be heard in the heat of battle. This particular French lad was attached to the 1st Regiment of the Light Infantry. The French troops had been waiting to fight since dawn and were beginning to discuss the possible reasons for the delay. The boy was longing for the action to start so that he could beat his drum while his comrades marched to victory. He was proud to be wearing his uniform of a blue jacket decorated with silver lace, and the shako he had kept dry in a water-proof cover during the night. It went without saying that his own side would win. Was not Napoleon's army the most famous in the world? He was still glowing from the morning's review when the troops had shouted and sung in the presence of their beloved Emperor.

Napoleon was in the green, white and gold uniform of a colonel of the Chasseurs à Cheval of the Imperial Guard with white breeches and high black riding boots. On top he wore his shabby old grey coat. On his head was the familiar black hat worn with the points to the sides. Paintings of Napoleon at the Battle of Waterloo always show him riding a white charger but he rode three horses that day – Marie and the greys Desireé and Marengo. Marengo was captured after the battle and his skeleton is exhibited today in the National Army Museum. Had the drummer boy been more experienced or had he a closer look he might have been shocked at the appearance of his Emperor. Napoleon had aged and grown stout. His cheeks were sunken and his complexion yellow. He was not nearly as fit as Wellington. He was feeling ill, exhausted and dozy. Napoleon, who had eaten a leisurely breakfast off silver plate in the inn called Le Caillou, had been in no hurry to start the battle, although some of his marshals were fretful at the delay. He had shown his contempt for his opponents by declaring, "I tell you, Wellington is a bad general, the English are bad troops, and this affair is nothing more than eating breakfast."

Having given battle orders to his marshals, he stayed back behind the French lines for the duration of the battle, first at Rossomme and then later at La Belle Alliance. His plan was simple. First there was to be an artillery bombardment to soften up the enemy. Then Ney was to lead a frontal attack with two infantry corps one on either side of the main road. This was to be followed by the advance of the cavalry and the Imperial Guard. There were to be no outflanking movements. However, three important factors threw a spanner in the works. One was that an attack intended as a diversion, was made on Hougoumont by Napoleon's younger brother Prince Jerome Bonaparte that lasted all day, sucking in more and more troops. In effect it became a battle within a battle.

Secondly, the main battle, planned to start early was delayed for hours because of the weather. Thirdly, Napoleon was late in discovering that the Prussians had recovered enough from their earlier defeat to be making their way westwards from Wavre to join Wellington.

It was nearly midday when Prince Jerome Bonaparte gave the signal for the 6th Infantry Division to advance on Hougoumont. The drummer boy began beating out the rhythm of a steady march on his drum, while the soldiers stepped out eagerly in the direction of the enemy. His hero Lieutenant Legros was well up in front with the 1st regiment. He was a powerful man known as 'L'enfonceur' (the enforcer) formerly an engineer who had risen up through the ranks. The boy fixed his eyes on the broad back ahead of him and was filled with courage. The soldiers, in massed formation, made their way through fields planted with tall wheat. The land dipped and curved to such an extent that they did not get a clear view of Hougoumont until they were very close to it. The first obstacles in their way were trees, for the château was surrounded on three sides by a thick wood and an orchard. From these trees they were receiving terrible punishment from volleys of musket shot. At the same time, shells were falling into their midst from well-placed British batteries of Horse Artillery above them.

Though the French were falling to the ground in hundreds the attack did not slacken. And the on-coming troop scrambled over dead or wounded comrades. They broke up their formation and poured into the wood and orchard where they had running fights with the British Redcoats and Dutch Greencoats, who fell back from tree to tree, firing as they went. By this time the drummer boy should have dropped back because no one expected an unarmed lad to

HOUGOUMONT

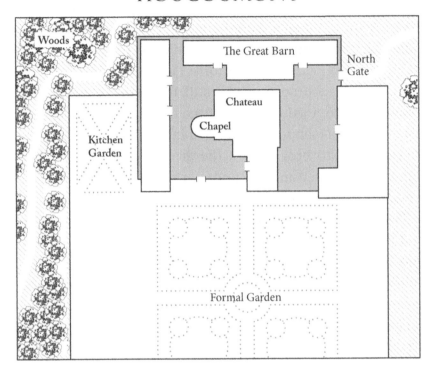

get mixed up in such an action, but somehow, he had got caught up in the attack and there was no turning back now. He stuck close to Legros and emerged from the wood unscathed.

The next obstacle to confront the French was a high brick wall. The château and farm buildings were enclosed within a walled courtyard giving on to a large walled garden. The whole complex resembled a small fortress and was being defended like one. As the French swarmed round the wall they were fired upon by the defenders, who were shooting from loopholes and platforms behind the walls. Many of the attackers were picked off and fell on top of the dead and wounded at the foot of the wall.

But they came on in overwhelming numbers, pushing back the Dutch and British soldiers who were still outside the walls. Reinforcements were being sent down from the Allied ridge and the French in their turn were pushed back. The fighting continued back and forth along the walls for a long time. In due course the boy, still following Legros, found himself on the northern side of the courtyard outside a huge gateway. Some sappers of the 1st Light Infantry were already there, trying to break down the great wooden door. Legros impatiently seized an axe and started to hack at the heavy wooden panels with savage strength.

The boy watched in wonder as the wood began to splinter and break. Legros and the sappers put their shoulders to the gate and slowly, slowly pushed the panels inward. The French soldiers behind them gave a roar of approval and surged through the opening into the courtyard. The boy, thrust forward in the press of bodies, suddenly found himself standing in the courtyard up against a little brick tower enclosing a well.

He shrank up against it and watched with growing terror the scene around him. The defenders and blue-coated invaders were fighting to the death in hand-to-hand combat with bayonets, rifle butts and axes. He saw a Nassauer officer being chased by a Frenchman who cut his hand off with an axe. He saw one Guardsman guzzling gin before rushing back into the fray. Those Frenchmen who had broken loose were being shot down by marksmen who were leaning out of the buildings within the courtyard. The boy looked towards the gate in the hope of seeing more French coming to the rescue. Instead he saw an enormous British officer, and a handful of guardsmen straining to get the door shut.

Macdonnell had realized that the gate must be closed at any

cost. Yelling at nearby soldiers to help him he dashed towards the gate. Sergeants Fraser, McGregor, and Aston together with Corporals James and Joseph Graham heaved on the gates until they were closed and barricaded shut. At this point all the invaders were overwhelmed. The boy gazed at the dead and mutilated bodies strewn around. Legros was sprawled face downwards with the axe still in his hands. The boy's legs turned to jelly and he sat down on the ground with a bump. Then it was he noticed that his drum had been torn off the strap that passed round his neck. It was all too much for him and he started to cry.

Someone helped him to his feet and he looked up to see a British soldier bending over him. He shrank back in terror, but the man said something in a friendly voice and smiled. The boy allowed himself to be led across to the château, up some stairs and into a room where wounded soldiers were laid out on the floor. A man in ordinary clothes was giving them water to drink, and to the boys' astonishment he spoke French. It turned out that he was a Belgian called Van Cutsem. He was the gardener at Hougoumont and his concern for his beautiful garden had led him to stay behind when all the other local inhabitants had moved away before the battle. Not that there was anything he could do to save his garden now.

Von Cutsem enlisted the boy's help in his task of giving water to the wounded who tended to be agonizingly parched. He sent the drummer boy down to the well in the courtyard to get more water. He found it difficult to concentrate on what he was doing because there was so much happening in the courtyard. He had never seen fighting like this before. Guardsmen were darting from place to place firing their muskets over the walls, out of windows and through loopholes. The boy could hear his own countrymen hammering on the main gate while the same corporal as before continued the work of shoring it up from inside. All of a sudden a French Grenadier who must have been standing on the shoulders of a comrade peered over the wall and took aim at Corporal James Graham who calmly took up his musket and shot him dead first.

Hardly had the boy taken in this astonishing scene when he heard a commotion on the opposite side of the courtyard. There were sounds of fighting outside, then a side door near the stables opened and more Foot Guards rushed in. The defenders were as delighted to see them as he was disappointed. He had hoped to see Frenchmen. The boy's attention was next caught by some casks that came flying over the wall. He ducked instinctively, thinking that they were going to explode, and was amazed to see the British falling on them with delight. They were cartridges. A supply wagon must have driven right to the base of the wall in order to keep the defenders in ammunition. The boy realized then that the French were not the only courageous ones. The British were brave too.

5

Lord William Lennox as Observer

Meanwhile William Lennox and his father, the Duke of Richmond, were making their way to the battlefield. They had decided to be where the action was even if they could not fight. As they rode southwards from Brussels they often had to leave the main road and take to the fields because the road was choked with traffic. When they passed through the village of Waterloo they spotted Lord Uxbridge, Wellington's Second-in-Command, who greeted them cheerfully with the words, "We shall have some sharp work today." Many senior officers had slept in the village the night before. 'His Grace the Duke of Wellington' was chalked up on the door of the inn, and other familiar names were to be seen on cottage doors.

When they reached the ridge of Mont St Jean they made their way to the right wing of the line where they had a chat with Major-General Maitland, who was commanding the 1st Infantry Brigade. He informed them that Hougoumont was being very hard pressed by the French, who greatly outnumbered the defenders, but he had confidence that the Guards under the command of Colonel James McDonnell would hold out. Wellington too had expressed his confidence when he had gone down earlier in the day to inspect the defences. Baron von Müffling (the Prussian representative) had been doubtful that the buildings could be held by so few men. "Ah!" replied Wellington. "But you don't know Macdonnell."

Mention of Wellington put the Duke and his son in mind that it was time they paid him their compliments, so they rode back along the ridge in search of him. They found him at the crossroads under an elm tree that had become his headquarters. Wellington was attending to the minutest details. He had a portfolio of pen, ink and paper in place of the pistol holder on his saddle. His aides stood close by in readiness to carry his written or verbal orders to any place they were needed. He frequently put a telescope to his eye and scanned the battlefield. The Duke was not overjoyed to see his visitors and greeted them sharply with the words, "William, you ought to be in bed; Duke you have no business here."

In fact, he was in a remarkably good humour. After a light breakfast of tea and toast at six o'clock he had been up and about directing operations himself, talking to his officers, and showing himself to his soldiers. As far as he was concerned the day was going well. Although the French were massed on the opposite ridge, it was nearly one o'clock and the main attack had not yet begun. He could see that the attack on Hougoumont, intended as a diversion, was using up more and more French soldiers, while he was keeping the number of defenders down to a minimum.

Every hour gained was to his advantage. The sun was out and the ground was drying rapidly. More importantly, he was expecting the Prussian army to arrive at any minute. Messengers had been passing between Wavre and Waterloo (a distance of only fourteen miles) and Wellington had made it clear that he would fight provided that he received some support from the Prussians. Trusty old Blücher had promised to bring up his army himself, although he had been wounded and trampled on at Ligny the day before.

The main French attack started at one p.m. by which time Lennox and his father had crossed over the chaussée to where the infantry was assembled in the left-centre of the line. In the first stage of the attack the French turned the full force of about eighty cannon on the Allied line. The noise of the cannon firing in unison was so shattering that Lennox's first inclination was to clap his hands over his ears. He was not able to do so because he was trying to keep his horse steady with his only good arm. Somehow he managed to keep control of himself and his horse. His father noticed and was pleased. "I am glad to see you stand your fire so well," he commented.

Wellington had instructed his soldiers to lie down behind the ridge where the slope offered some protection from the missiles, and the soft ground prevented them from ricocheting. Even so, the solid balls were maiming and killing at

FRENCH 6-POUNDER CANNON

random and in the most horrible way. A brigade of Dutch-Belgians was having a particularly bad time of it. For some reason they were positioned in front of the road rather than behind it, and in traditional continental style they had chosen to stand up rather than lie down in the face of fire, with the result that they were being knocked down like ninepins.

But if the French thought the fearful cannonading would break down the spirit of their opponents they were wrong. On the whole, the soldiers remained remarkably cool under fire. Young Lennox noticed how they carried on talking and joking as if nothing out of the ordinary was happening. He became quite nonchalant himself and moved around talking to the officers he knew by name, many of whom he had last seen in his house on the night of 15 June.

He spoke to Sir Thomas Picton, the divisional commander, who was rather curiously dressed for battle in a top hat and frock coat. He had been in the thick of the fighting at Quatre Bras and did not look well but his manner was as blunt and genial as usual. Lennox offered his sympathy to Sir Denis Pack who had lost so many of his fine Scottish soldiers at Quatre Bras. If these officers were surprised at seeing him wandering about the battlefield with one arm in a sling and a bandage over one eye they were too polite to say so.

After half an hour the cannonading suddenly stopped and William felt a great sense of relief. He had gone slightly deaf and his good eye was watering from the acrid black smoke. Then he noticed that the soldiers around him had fallen silent. They were checking their weapons with tense looks on their faces. They knew what was coming. He knew too when he felt the ground vibrating with the measured tread of thousands and thousands of soldiers marching towards them.

Lennox urged his horse up the slope to get a better view. What he saw through the cloud of black smoke made him gasp. The disciplined French soldiers were coming across the valley in dense masses or columns that looked as if they would carry all before them. He had heard some veterans predict that the French formations would be clumsy under fire, but they looked very impressive to him as they came on unopposed. Out in front, the Dutch-Belgian brigade turned tail and fled. They had already suffered greatly in the earlier cannonading. As they fled through the British ranks on their way to the rear they were booed and hissed and helped on their way with bayonet thrusts and a few musket shots.

Lennox kept his eyes fixed on Sir Thomas Picton, who was up on the ridge waiting for the right moment to order his men to spring up and advance. When the French were very close, Picton gave the order to fire and the red-coated soldiers in their muddied uniforms and crumpled black shakos, the Gordons and the Black Watch in their bonnets and kilts sprang up along the ridge and let off their muskets. The kilted warriors looked so terrifying they were nicknamed 'ladies from hell.' Then Picton raised his sword and shouted, "Charge! Hurrah! Hurrah!" No sooner were the words out of his mouth than Lennox saw him pitch on to the neck of his horse. A musket ball had entered his temple. His soldiers carried him off the field. But the British infantrymen had obeyed his order and were engaged in hand-to-hand fighting with their bayonets.

At this stage Lord Uxbridge sent the British heavy cavalry to help the infantry regiments. They came down in grand style from their position in the rear. Lennox had to rein in his own horse as the Royals, the Scots Greys and the Irish Inniskillings of the Union Brigade pushed past on huge grey horses. They were led by Sir William Ponsonby who was mounted on a rather poor-looking hack he was riding so as to save his own fine horse. The horsemen scrambled up the ridge, jumped the hedges of the road and set themselves at the enemy. Lennox heard his father shouting, "Go along, my boys now's your time" to the Irishmen as they tore past

When the 'heavies' were gone and the way was clear, Lennox spurred his horse to the top of the ridge from where he saw an incredible sight. The French were in disarray. As the veterans had predicted, they had found it impossible to manoeuvre. The men behind them were floundering uselessly in the mud. Some were trying to flee, some were laying down their weapons and trying to surrender. Others were fighting their own comrades in an effort to find a way back to their lines. A huge British sergeant called Charles Ewart was seen carrying a French standard off the battlefield. The standard with its golden eagle had been wrested away from the 45th, the 'invincibles' of the French army. To win it Ewart had to kill three French soldiers with his slashing sword. Large numbers of prisoners were being escorted to the rear.

But then Lennox heard the shrill notes of the bugles sounding the rally and he knew that the cavalry was out of control. The horsemen were charging right across the valley, up the slope and into the French lines. They were too far away and too excited to pay attention to the calls for their return. They were in among the cannon that had caused the punishing bombardment earlier on. They were cut off from Lennox's view by a huge body of French cavalry who appeared to surround them. Some of the French cavalry carried long lances as weapons. The British cavalry did not use the lance that they now learnt was a lethal weapon capable of doing terrible harm. If the allied light cavalry from the left wing had not rushed to help them there might have been no survivors at all.

These came straggling back in ones and twos. Some of them were on foot, some were slumped on the backs of horses. Many horses came back without riders and both men and beasts were covered with lance wounds. In one way the charge had been very successful. Two eagles had been captured, many guns put out of action, and thousands of prisoners taken. But the losses had been fearful. They included Sir William Ponsonby who had been seen lying dead on the field beside his hired hack. It did not seem likely that the shrunken Union Brigade would be able to do anything useful again that day.

Lennox suddenly felt very exhausted and shaken. His injured eye was throbbing painfully and his senses were reeling from what he had witnessed. He was also deaf from the earlier cannonading. He could hardly take in the devastation around him. French muskets had been left behind in rows in the bloodstained rye. Men and horses lay scattered over the valley, not all of them were dead. It was getting on for three o'clock and a fresh bombardment had started. When his father suggested that it was time to go home, Lennox did not disagree. The battle was altogether more than he had bargained for.

6

The Von Ompteda Boys

———⟨⟨⟨⟨⟨⟩⟩⟩⟩⟩———

Two young Germans were involved in the centre of the battlefield. Christian and Louis Von Ompteda were there by chance. They had come out to Belgium in the spring of 1815 to join their uncle, Colonel Christian Von Ompteda, who was in command of the 1st and 2nd Light Battalions, and the 5th and 8th Line Battalions of the King's German Legion – over a thousand men. They were attached to their uncle's regiment, the 5th Line Battalion, on a temporary basis while their own regiment, the 6th Line, was in Sicily. They wore scarlet jackets like the British and had been trained in a similar way.

Christian, who was seventeen, had been in the KGL for three years already, and Louis, who was fifteen, for one year. The boys were carrying on a family tradition by becoming soldiers. Not only was their uncle an officer in the KGL but their father was one too. Both men had come over to England as exiles when Hanover was overrun by Napoleon and had dedicated their lives to building up the KGL into the success-ful fighting force it had become.

Although a bachelor, Colonel Von Ompteda was a devoted family man and he was delighted when his nephews came out to join him. He was much concerned at their lack of education, and spent his spare time giving them lessons, for he himself was a cultivated man. Some time in May while the boys were still with their uncle, they received the sad and unexpected news of their father's death. Now that he was responsible for them, Colonel Von Ompteda thought it his duty to send them home to Hanover to study. Before the arrangements could be completed, however, Napoleon had crossed the border, the KGL was set in motion, and Von Ompteda had no choice but to take the boys along.

Christian and Louis knew that their presence on the battlefield worried their uncle, yet they could not help being relieved at the way things had turned out, because they had not wanted to go home. They had been brought up as soldiers in a unit that had dedicated itself to the defeat of Napoleon. They had not seen action at Quatre Bras, and now they had a chance to fight, they were glad not to be missing it.

Wellington had shown his confidence in the KGL by placing it in the right-centre of the line. The 2nd Light Battalion under the command of Major Baring had been entrusted with the defence of La Haye Sainte. To start with they numbered some 400 men only. Behind the farm was the 1st Light Battalion, while the 5th Line Battalion, to which the boys were attached, and the 8th Line Battalion were positioned behind the ridge at the crossroads. As brigade commander, Colonel Von Ompteda was responsible for them all. Early that morning in the company of his nephews he had inspected each position for himself.

He had not been very satisfied with the defences in the farm house of La Haye Sainte. The pioneers of the battalion, who carried tools, had been sent over to help with the defences of Hougoumont, with the result that very little had

La Haye Sainte

been done at La Haye Sainte. A barricade had been built across the chaussée, and some loopholes had been knocked into the wall overlooking the road, rather feeble defences for a stronghold that was in such a vital position between the two sides.

The men were in good spirits mainly because they had spent a comfortable night in comparison to their comrades outside. They had been dry and had kept themselves warm with a huge bonfire that they had fed with wooden shutters and barn doors. They had found plenty to eat from the kitchen garden and the orchard. Although they were only some four hundred men in total they had been confident that they could hold the farmhouse especially as their old companions in arms, the 95th Rifles, were posted in the sandpit on the hillock opposite.

Because of its prominent position, the KGL was under pressure from the moment the main French attack started. Christian and Louis had their first taste of cannonading and did not like it. But they kept calm, and as chance would have it, were not hit by the deadly missiles. Neither did they like standing still while the French infantry bore down upon them. To keep their nerves steady they kept their eyes on their uncle who was mounted on a horse out in front. The French came steadily on. They pushed the 95th Rifles out of the sandpit, and like an army of ants engulfing a morsel of food, they surrounded the small farmhouse. Only then did Von Ompteda order the 8th Line to advance.

Christian and Louis watched with admiration as their comrades stepped forward eagerly to meet the enemy. They cheered out loud when they saw them falling upon the opposing Frenchmen with their bayonets fixed in their muskets. The Redcoats seemed to be making some headway when all of a sudden a body of French Cuirassiers appeared on the scene. These famous French cavalrymen were a daunting sight. Picked for their size, they looked even more gigantic in shining steel helmets and breastplates. With their slashing swords they cut the 8th Line to pieces.

When Von Ompteda ordered the 5th Line to advance, the soldiers marched forward without hesitation, although they had seen what had happened to the 8th Line. Christian and Louis went with them. It was now that the months of drill and training they had undergone in the army stood them in good stead. The only time they faltered was when they saw their uncle fall from his horse. But they pressed on again when they saw him scramble to his feet. He had a set look on his face as he continued on foot to meet his fate. He did not know that help was close at hand in the shape of the Household Cavalry sent to the rescue at the same time as the Union Brigade had swept past Lennox on the other side of the cross-roads. Lord Uxbridge himself was leading the charge with cries of "To Paris!"

It gave Christian and Louis a tremendous thrill to see the tall soldiers in their crested helmets and flowing plumes surging past on their black horses. They caught sight of the boy bugler John Edwards who had sounded the charge. The Horse Guards fell upon the Cuirassiers like avenging angels, their swords making a terrific clattering sound on their opponents' breastplates and helmets. The French infantry, surprised by the cavalry attack, lost their formation and withdrew to their own lines in total confusion. Unfortunately, the Household Brigade, like the Union Brigade, did not know when to stop. They went right into the enemy guns where most of them were slaughtered. Young John Edwards was one of the few lucky ones to return.

Although the enemy had been repulsed, there was little rejoicing in the KGL. Von Ompteda was stricken by his heavy losses. The 8th Line had lost its commander, seven officers, and over a hundred men. It had also lost its colour, which was considered a particular disgrace. The news from La Haye Sainte was less depressing, for the defenders had managed to keep the French out of the farm buildings. A fire which had broken out in the barn had been put out with water from the pond carried in camp kettles along a human chain. For the moment, the main problem in the farmhouse seemed to be a shortage of ammunition.

When Von Ompteda received the request for more ammunition he sent a messenger to the rear to bring up an ammunition wagon. He could not lay his hands on any of the reserves already on the field because many of the KGL used a different sort of weapon from the rest of British army. The standard British gun was a musket, known affectionately as 'Brown Bess.' It was not very accurate and was extremely heavy to handle but the troops liked it. The crackshot Rifle

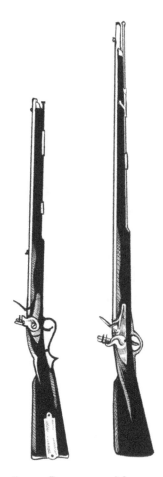

BAKER RIFLE   MUSKET

Brigades and some of the KGL had been given a more accurate weapon called the Baker Rifle that had a longer range and was more accurate. It was the reserve ammunition for the Baker, which for some reason was lacking.

The French had suffered badly too. Christian and Louis could see wounded men in the mangled rye who were still defiantly called out the name of their Emperor. In the lull that followed the attack, they witnessed another act of courage. A solitary horseman rode right up to La Haye Sainte. Since he was alone it was presumed that he was a deserter come to give himself up, so no one shot at him. He rode up to the barriers in the road, stood up in his stirrups to see over it, waved his sword and shouted "Vive l'Empereur." Only when he was galloping back to his lines did the marksmen try unsuccessfully to shoot him down.

Although some of their comrades were talking as if the battle was all but won, the Von Ompteda boys were not reassured by their uncle. He looked very worried indeed. So did Wellington. They saw him quite clearly when he came to the crossroads to see to the strengthening of La Haye Sainte. He had an abstracted look of concentration on his face and seemed hardly aware of the men surrounding him. He spoke only to deliver an order, and he kept looking anxiously through his glass in the direction in which he expected the Prussians to appear. It was three o'clock and there was still no sign of them.

7

William Leeke and the French Cavalry Charge

⸻ ∘⊙∘ ⸻

Shortly after three o'clock William Leeke's battalion, the 52nd was ordered out of its reserve position and the crack regiment moved forward with drilled precision. By this time William Leeke had grown used to cannon fire. He had even had a narrow escape himself when a piece of shell had entered the knapsack upon which he had been resting his head. Sergeant Rhodes had calmly extracted the fragment from among the mess tins with the words, "if that had hit either you or me on the head sir, I think it would have settled our business for us."

In spite of this experience Leeke was totally unprepared for what was in store for him. As they left the shelter of the ridge he saw two soldiers of the 52nd lying dead under a tree and he could not keep back his tears. There was a moment of light relief when an officer called Cottingham was wounded in the ankle by a spent cannon ball. Cottingham was rather a figure of fun in the regiment because of a habit he had of saying "By Jove, by Jove!" Leeke found himself laughing now when he saw Cottingham hopping up and down on one foot exclaiming, "oh by Jove, by Jove!" There was nothing funny though about the heap of dead and wounded Brunswickers that Leeke saw next. One of them who had had his leg shot off at the thigh caught hold of the hand of a British soldier before falling down dead. Leeke was deeply moved by the sight.

As they marched forward they came level with Hougoumont which was now in a dire situation. Falling shells had started a fire and it looked as if every building was ablaze. Flames were shooting up from the roof and black smoke was pouring out of the courtyard. It did not seem possible that they could hold out much longer.

When the soldiers were well out in front of the Allied line they stopped and formed two squares. A square was made by four ranks of men facing outwards in four straight lines that met at the corners. When a square was under attack from cavalry the men in the front rank knelt down and stuck the butts of their muskets in the ground so that the sharp points of the bayonets were pointing upwards. The second rank crouched low with their bayonet tips not far behind those in front. The two ranks behind stood upright with their muskets ready and loaded. The centre of the square was occupied by an assistant surgeon, the wounded and officers mounted on horseback. These officers gave orders and encouraged the soldiers but did not handle the guns themselves. Gaps in the front row were filled from the rows behind.

Leeke, still holding the colour, found himself in the fourth line of the front face of the square that was being treated to a fearsome cannonading. The French had trained their guns on to the Allied right wing and the 52nd in its exposed position in front of the ridge received more than its fair share of shot, shell, and canister. Leeke was so terrified he tried to distract himself by playing a little game. He started to track the course of the missiles that were flying around. He found that

A SQUARE

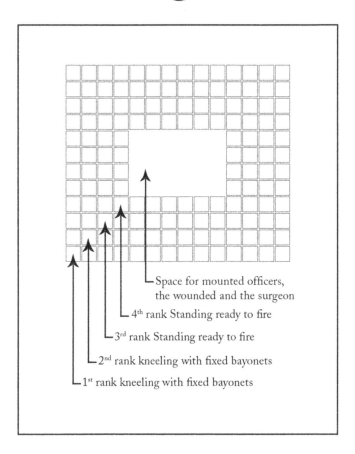

Space for mounted officers,
the wounded and the surgeon

4th rank Standing ready to fire

3rd rank Standing ready to fire

2nd rank kneeling with fixed bayonets

1st rank kneeling with fixed bayonets

it was easier to see objects that were being shot towards the enemy from the ridge behind him than objects that were coming towards him. In addition to the crashing boom of the cannon as they fired, Leeke became aware of another sound – a sort of humming whizzing noise made by missiles as they flew overhead.

He had been playing this game for a while when a shaft of sunlight highlighted some brass guns on the French side. He could see them quite clearly, and as if in a trance he watched them being loaded up and fired. He saw a cannon ball coming straight towards the middle of the square, straight towards him.

His first impulse was to move out of the way. But it was considered cowardly for an officer to duck, so he drew himself up straight and waited for what he knew must happen. In fact, the cannon ball went through the front face of the square a little to the right of Leeke. It passed within two inches of the colour pole in his right hand and skimmed over the rear face of the square without doing any further damage. Two of the men who had been hit had fallen dead outside the square. In the centre of the square the surgeon was dressing wounds and even performing amputations. Any dead soldiers in the centre were thrown outside to make room for the wounded.

A wounded man was groaning a great deal until an officer asked him kindly not to make so much noise. Leeke realized then that apart from Cottingham's "By Jove!" and the outcry of this man he had not heard the wounded make any noise. This surprised him because he had been told to expect unnerving cries on the battlefield. The cannonading though was far worse than he had been led to believe. To stand up defenceless before cannon shot was a terrible strain on the nerves. Everyone was glad when the firing stopped, even though it meant that an attack on foot and horse was imminent.

When the attack came it quite took Leeke's breath away. He saw the French cavalry coming in waves across the valley. They came in their thousands at a steady trot, the most famous horsemen in the world, led by Ney, the 'bravest of the brave' of all French commanders. In the lead were the terrifying Cuirassiers. Over six foot tall and mounted on huge horses these cavalry men in their steel helmets with flowing plumes and shiny steel breastplates were intimidating. Next came the Lancers in bright red and green uniforms, the flags on their deadly weapons fluttering in the breeze. They were followed by the Chasseurs of the Guard in green and gold uniforms and tall black bearskins.

The order rang out for the Allied line to "prepare to receive cavalry" and within seconds, Leeke's square had formed its barrier of bristling steel. To Leeke it seemed certain that the square would be washed away by the advancing waves. But the veterans were chuckling with delight. Napoleon must have taken leave of his senses because it was madness to send up cavalry alone against infantry. If the square kept steady no harm could come to it. It seemed hard to believe, but Leeke could already see what terrible damage the Allied guns were doing to the advancing horsemen. The gunners had been ordered not to fire until the last possible moment when they should run back behind the ridge for protection carrying a wheel of the gun with them so that it could not be carried off by the French.

It was the Cuirassiers who were bearing down on Leek's square. They had broken into a gallop and looked very formidable, but they went down like ninepins when the ranks of the square fired their muskets. Some were killed or wounded. Others were prevented by their breastplates from getting up easily. The rest set themselves at the square, but at the last minute their horses, terrified by the bayonets, sheered away and passed along the sides of the square, suffering badly from the hail of bullets they received.

They galloped up to the ridge where they reformed before coming back down on to the rear face of the square. Again they did not dare to attack but veered off to the sides. When they returned to their own lines they left heaps of dead and wounded men and horses in their wake.

By this time all the men who handled muskets in Leek's square looked like chimney sweeps. Their faces had become blackened in the complicated process of reloading their muskets. Each soldier carried sixty cartridges in a leather pouch at his waist. A cartridge consisted of a piece of waxed paper twisted at both ends around loose gunpowder and a small spherical lead musket ball. At close range it could be lethal. To remove the contents the soldiers bit off one end of cartridge paper and poured some of the powder into the pan and the rest into the barrel of their muskets. They then bit off the other end, took the ball between their teeth and spat it into the barrel. They screwed up the paper and stuffed it down on top of the powder and ball. When the trigger was pulled the gunpowder in the pan was ignited which set off the charge that expelled the bullet. This constant movement meant that the soldiers' faces become black and their mouths gritty and parched. Over time their teeth became worn down and broken.

As soon as the French were back on their side the dreaded cannon fire started up again. The noise, smoke and effects of the firing were so unpleasant that Leeke was relieved when another cavalry attack started. The cavalry came up seven or eight times in all so that Leeke began to recognize some of his opponents and to feel personally hostile towards them. Some of the soldiers around him were pulling faces at the enemy. The British soldiers could not understand why the French command did not send infantry and mobile guns to support the cavalry who looked terrifying but could not break the squares. Neither could the French cavalry commanders understand why Ney insisted they charge over and over again without support.

Towards six o'clock the attacks began to slacken and eventually they stopped altogether. Ney had had five horses shot under him and had been seen beating an abandoned British cannon with his sword out of sheer frustration. Wellington had been seen all along the ridge encouraging the men to stand firm. He probably rode some thirty miles during the battle on his sturdy horse Copenhagen who never faltered. Some squares had wavered, but not one had broken.

8

The Von Ompteda Boys and the Fall of La Haye Sainte

———❧—————

In the centre of the line the Von Ompteda boys were subjected to the same cavalry attacks as Leeke and reacted to them in much the same way. They discovered to their surprise that the 5th Line Battalion in square was more than a match for the awesome cavalry. They also came to dread the intervals when the cavalry withdrew and the cannonading started. They would not have admitted it but they were glad of the company of their uncle. Von Ompteda, still on foot remained in the centre of the 5th Line square throughout the afternoon. In his heavily accented English he kept up the morale of his men with constant words of encouragement.

In the intervals between attacks the Cuirassiers who were attacking the 5th Line square did not return to their ridge, but retired into a protective dip out of reach of musket shot. To make matters worse, one of their officers took to riding up and down on some high ground in full view of the square. Von Ompteda became more and more irritated by the arrogance of this man until at last he begged someone in the square to get rid of him. One after another the soldiers took aim and fired. Every shot missed and the French officer looked upon the square with more disdain than ever.

A sharpshooter from the 1st Light Battalion who had been brought wounded into the square offered to have a go. Although he had a smashed leg and was faint from loss of blood he was carried in a blanket to the front of the square. Somehow he raised himself up, took aim and killed the Frenchman with a single shot. Christian and Louis joined in the hearty cheer that greeted his effort.

Towards six o'clock when the cavalry attacks on the right wing had tailed off, the pressure on the centre was increased. Napoleon had ordered La Haye Sainte to be captured at all costs and Ney renewed the attack with a combined force of infantry, cavalry and artillery. The defenders in the farmhouse, reinforced by two light companies of Dutchmen, had so far kept the French at bay. But for some reason, the fresh supplies of ammunition that had been sent for had not arrived and each man was now down to his last cartridges.

The boys knew that a crisis point had been reached when their uncle mounted a dead officer's horse and rode out of the square, leaving it in the charge of Lieutenant-Colonel Linsingen. With deep concern Von Ompteda was watching a thousand French infantrymen converging on La Haye Sainte. What tactics he would have used against them no one was ever to know for at that moment the 1st Corps Commander, the Prince of Orange, decided to interfere.

He sent an aide over to Von Ompteda with an order for him to advance against the approaching infantry. Christian and Louis, who were straining their ears to hear the exchange, heard their uncle reply that he was most reluctant to move his battalions forward without cavalry support. He also pointed out the crests of some Cuirassiers who were hiding in the hollow in front. The aide rode away with the message, whereupon the Prince of Orange himself came up.

When the Prince's orders were repeated, Von Ompteda went white with anger and the boys knew that he was keeping himself under control with the greatest difficulty. He replied that he thought such an advance would be mistaken because they would be set upon by the French cavalry who were just visible in the hollow. The Prince studied the tips of the helmets and announced that they belonged to his own Dutch troops. This was too much for the colonel who contradicted him. The Prince was not accustomed to being answered back and he did not like it. Neither did he like to admit that he was wrong. So he drew himself up haughtily and said, "I must still repeat my order to attack in line with the bayonet, and I will listen to no further arguments."

The boys were aghast. What was their uncle going to do now? If he disobeyed the orders he would be punished for disobedience or cowardice. Von Ompteda hesitated for a moment before saying in a loud voice, "Well, I will." He had answered defiantly, but then he knew, and his soldiers knew, and Christian and Louis knew, that they had been ordered to their deaths. Von Ompteda drew his sword, turned to face his troops and ordered them to deploy into line. The last words he spoke concerned his nephews. Turning to Linsingen he said, "Try and save my two nephews." Then he wheeled his horse round and cantered off alone in front of his men.

As if in a nightmare the boys found themselves marching forward with their comrades. Within minutes the Cuirassiers were upon them. They had been waiting, as Von Ompteda had guessed, for the chance to pounce. They laid into the helpless foot soldiers with their vicious swords. Christian and Louis stuck close together waiting to be struck down. All around them men were groaning as they fell, horses were whinnying with fright and bayonets were clashing against swords. They had seen Linsingen and his horse crashing to the ground and felt very much alone in the confusion.

Suddenly Linsingen popped up beside them. His horse had fallen on top of him but he had escaped injury. He seized the boys by the arms and dragged them through the fray to the dip that had sheltered the enemy so well earlier on. There they found other survivors of the regiment. The boys were anxious to leave the shelter to search for their uncle, but Linsingen restrained them. He reminded them of their uncle's last words and begged them to remain where they were.

When the boys finally reached the safety of the ridge they learnt that La Haye Sainte had fallen. The last straw was when they ran out of ammunition. The survivors were coming back in ones and twos with horrendous tales of what had happened. When their cartridges had finally given out they had been unable to stop the French pouring into the farmhouse. They had defended themselves in hand-to-hand combat with rifles and bayonets in the rooms and passage-ways until they were killed or managed to escape across the fields at the back. One example of the sort of fighting they had been engaged in was experienced by a skirmisher called Frederick Lindau. Early on in the fighting he had riffled the pockets of a dead French officer and found a bag of gold. Then he spent his time in the barn calmly shooting at the French trying to come in by the door. He was wounded in the head twice but continued to fight despite blood pouring down his face through a bandage. Baring told him to withdraw to have his wounds dressed but he refused saying, "He would be a scoundrel that deserted you, so long as his head is on his shoulders."

One young lieutenant told of how he had actually been captured, but seeing that the faces of the Frenchmen were as white and frightened as his own, he succeeded in breaking loose from them. Major Baring, the officer in charge of La Haye Sainte, also came back alive. Nobody held out any hope for Von Ompteda and before long the boys learnt the circumstances of his death.

The officer who had been the last man to see him alive told the boys what he had seen as he galloped behind Von Ompteda towards the French and La Haye Sainte. He had noticed that although the French had their muskets leveled at the colonel, they had not pulled the triggers. It was as if they were transfixed by the sight of a lone officer careering down upon them. Or perhaps they thought he had come to give himself up. The French officers had even struck the barrels of the mens' guns to prevent them from firing. Von Ompteda had reached the garden on the north side of La Haye Sainte and he had put his horse over the hedge. The enemy still appeared to be paralyzed by the sight of him, and he was able to strike left and right with his sword before he sank from his horse and vanished from sight.

No one could comfort the boys in their sorrow. The feeling of despair was general. Most of the soldiers in the KGL feared that the battle was lost. French skirmishers were now swarming all over the area between the farmhouse and the ridge. A cannon had been brought up to the knoll opposite La Haye Sainte to within one hundred yards of the Allied line. Many soldiers who had remained unharmed so far that day were killed or maimed now until the 95th Rifles succeeded in silencing the cannon.

When Wellington rode past, it was noted that he had very few aides-de-camp left. Without the presence of the Prussians he did not believe he could win the battle. Unfortunately because of the difficult terrain they had to cross to reach the Allied army at Waterloo the Prussians had still not yet arrived on the flank, though they had started a fierce struggle with the French in a village to the south-east. Wellington had no more reserves to throw in so he sent out word that the soldiers must now stand in their places until the last man fell.

9

Mary Adwicke and the Crisis in the Rear

⸻◦❦◦⸻

By seven o'clock the crisis at the front was being felt in the rear where Mary and her mother were to be found. They had settled down at Mont St Jean near the large walled farmhouse now serving as a field hospital manned by surgeons and their assistants. With the exception of the farmer's wife who was hiding in an attic, the local inhabitants had fled the place. Before leaving they had removed all their livestock except for the pigeons. They had bricked up the cellars, hidden their linen and valuables in barrels and buried their oil and vinegar. Their places had been taken by a dozen or so assistant surgeons and several hundred wounded.

A sure sign that things were not going well for the Allies was the increasing flow of wounded. More than 5,000 casualties ended up in the farmhouse. In addition to ordinary soldiers, a number of important officers were being brought in. The young Quarter-master-General, Sir William de Lancey, was a serious loss to Wellington. He had been struck a glancing blow by a cannon ball. He was taken into the farmhouse, but later removed to a humble cottage further back from the line.

Two of Wellington's favourite aides were wounded at around this time. Lord Fitzroy Somerset had been standing with his left arm touching Wellington's right arm when it was shot off. Sir Alexander Gordon had also been wounded so severely, that the surgeons at Mont St Jean could do nothing for him. After a while, he was moved to the inn at Waterloo where at least he could be more comfortable. The Prince of Orange was brought off the field with a wounded shoulder but was well enough to be transported to Brussels.

The wounded had overflowed from the farmhouse into the courtyard where they were lying around on beds of straw. The courage of the wounded was astonishing, Soldiers today would not be able to endure what they had to two hundred years ago. Operations were performed without anaesthetic. Wine and opium might be given after an operation but not during it. Those who had fought in the Peninsula had learnt from observation that immediate amputation often meant a better chance of survival and begged to be seen to without delay.

The surgeons, or 'chips' as they were affectionately called, could not work fast enough. There were never enough of them and they had far more casualties than they could cope with. Each surgeon had a wooden case of instruments containing knives, saws, scalpels, tourniquets, forceps and blades as well as lint for dressings, linen for bandages and silk for sewing wounds. With these instruments they were able to extract bullets, sew chest wounds, set fractures and amputate limbs. Three-quarters of the battle injuries were to limbs. They left stomach wounds untreated as these were usually fatal.

Amputation Saws

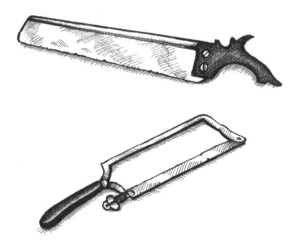

If their patients did not die of shock, they could get infections or gangrene because antibiotics and antiseptics had not yet been invented. The practice of bleeding (taking blood) from patients made things worse. Now and again the surgeons in their bloodied aprons came out into the courtyard for a breath of air, or to sharpen their instruments. They knew that they would still be working long after the battle was over. They did not even have time to bury amputated limbs that lay in gory piles where they operated. Mary and her mother had grown hardened to these sights. Indeed Mrs Adwicke was often called upon to lend a hand with the wounded.

Meanwhile, Mary was taking care of the baby outside the main gate. She was keeping a sharp lookout for her father in case he was brought in wounded. She knew that he would not be brought in dead, because if ordinary soldiers were killed they were left on the field until the battle was over. Only the bodies of officers, carried without the aid of stretchers, were brought to the rear if possible.

Those in the rear got what information they could from the bandsmen who brought in the wounded. When they had deposited their loads, they lingered on at the farmhouse, seeming in no hurry to get back to the scene of action. Then the camp followers crowded round and plied them with questions. By this time, many of them thought the Allies had lost the battle. One man swore that he had seen the Prussians arrive and then go away again. Others told of the capture of La Haye Sainte and the onslaught on the centre of the line.

Mary did not need the bandsmen to tell her that things were going badly. She could see for herself that a large number of soldiers were deserting the field. She knew that hundreds of them were hiding in the forest behind the farm because she had seen them lolling beside camp fires when she went in search of firewood. A great stir had been caused in the rear when an entire cavalry regiment had come cantering past. They had looked fresh and well turned out and did not appear to have been fighting. They were German troops, the Cumberland Hussars, and they had galloped through, shouting that the French had won and were in hot pursuit.

Some of the women were thrown into a panic and started back for Brussels. A few of the more hardy went forward in search of their menfolk. Some were weeping or drowning their sorrows in gin. Those who had been widowed were already discussing whom they would marry next. Unmarried women were not allowed in the army so they would have to act quickly if they were to remain. The children, in their bare feet, tattered dresses or cut-a-way uniforms, went on with what they were doing. Whether their fathers were dead or not, they still had to look after their little brothers and sisters and scavenge for food.

Every now and again Mary would dart into the road to pick up objects that caught her fancy. The road was cluttered with upturned carts and strewn with officers' baggage. It was also reeking of spilt gin. But she had to be very careful not to get trampled under foot because traffic was still passing to and fro. Carts were bringing up supplies and taking back those wounded fit enough to withstand the jolting of an unsprung vehicle all the way to Brussels. Only the French had specially designed vehicles to carry the wounded. These were light, well-sprung, horse-drawn carriages in which the wounded could be laid, and were known as 'flying ambulances'.

Mary was very tired. It seemed a long, long time since she had got up in the cold drizzly dawn. Her head was throbbing from the noise of cannon and she felt dazed by all the sights she had seen that day. At last, with the baby in her arms, she lay down where she was by the side of the road and went to sleep.

10

William Leeke in Pursuit
of the French

By this time, Leeke's 52nd had moved out of the direct line of fire and was sheltering behind the ridge again. Only Wellington and his aides knew how the entire battle was unfolding. Mostly the soldiers were only aware of what was happening immediately around them. Leeke did not know that La Haye Sainte had been taken, or that the centre of the line was in the gravest danger.

Leeke was thinking of the death of poor Ensign Nettles who had been killed outright in the company of his colour sergeant when the 52nd was moving backwards. He suddenly realized that if he had insisted on being sent to the left wing of the regiment he would be dead and Nettles would be still alive. Now he was grateful to be where he was, and grateful to have Sergeant Rhodes beside him. This kind man kept a watchful eye on him and prevented him from putting out his foot to stop a spent cannon ball,

Leeke noticed a tortoiseshell kitten lying dead a few yards away. He thought it must have been fleeing from Hougoumont when it was killed. The sight of such a homely object on the battlefield made him think of his family and friends in England. Fortunately, he was distracted from his homesick mood by the arrival of a Frenchman on horseback. This cavalry officer came galloping up to the 52nd shouting "Vive le Roi" to show that he was betraying the Emperor Napoleon. He told Sir John Colborne that Napoleon was preparing a last mighty attack with the Imperial Guard.

The news spread through the ranks like wildfire. Everyone knew that the Guard was the elite corps of the French army. These picked soldiers included an Old Guard of men with at least twelve years service. They got more pay and smarter uniforms than their comrades. They had their own medical service and special supplies so that they would not go hungry. Napoleon made no secret of his affection for them. He lavished medals on them and kept them in reserve if he could. Even when the battle was in the balance and Ney had sent to Napoleon for more reinforcements, the Emperor had snapped, "Troops? Where do you expect me to get them?" He would not spare his Guards even then. They always carried their dress uniforms in their packs so that they could lead the triumphal marches that followed upon Napoleon's victories. Even Leeke understood that in sending up his favorite troops, Napoleon was dealing his last and strongest card.

The news was immediately relayed to the Duke of Wellington who came down to where the 52nd was waiting just before eight o'clock. He rode along the line quite alone and stood talking to Sir John Colborne as they watched the movement of the enemy across the valley. Leeke noted with pride that Colborne was still wearing the cape and hood he had lent him. He was deeply impressed by Wellington's calm expression and the quiet way he rode away unattended. His plain blue uniform may well have stopped him being a target.

While the Guard, in massed columns, marched steadily into the valley between Hougoumont and La Haye Sainte, the 52nd and the rest of the brigade, of which it formed a unit, moved forward to meet them. Seeing an opportunity to strike the French on their right flank, Colborne (without waiting for orders from Wellington) instructed his regiment to swing itself round.

Leeke found himself giving three cheers at the top of his voice as his well-trained regiment made a right shoulders forward movement to get itself into line with the French flank. Colborne and other officers put themselves at the head of the four-deep line and called to the men to advance upon the enemy. One of the officers placed his cap on the point of his sword, stood up in his stirrups and gave a loud cheer. The next minute Leeke was moving forward with the standard in both hands.

While the French were being attacked from the right, they were receiving fierce fire from the British regiments in front and to the left of them. For a time the French veterans in the outer ranks returned the musket fire gallantly. Leeke saw his comrades falling left, right, and centre. Colborne had his horse shot under him but reappeared wiping his mouth with a white handkerchief. But suddenly the French broke under the British fire. They had not expected much trouble and were overcome by the force of the resistance.

To his amazement Leeke saw the columns start to disintegrate like cakes falling into crumbs. One minute he was looking down the barrels of muskets, the next he was staring at retreating packs. Napoleon's most famous soldiers were running away. It was unbelievable. Meanwhile the Prussians were pouring on to the field and Wellington knew that his moment had come.

He stood up in his stirrups beside the elm tree, took off his hat and waved it three times towards the French. His men understood the signal. They had been on the defensive all day and now longed to take the offensive. They cheered loudly and left the ridge. The 52nd was in the lead and Leeke got the distinct impression that his regiment had been responsible for the rout and was alone in the chase.

The field was now so dark and smoky that it was difficult to see what was happening. The uniforms on both sides had been so stained with mud and horse dung that distinguishing colours did not help. The sudden appearance of some cavalry men caused great confusion. Some of the soldiers of the 52nd opened up their ranks to let them through, but others, thinking that they were Frenchmen, started to shoot them down. Leeke tried to drag his sword out of its scabbard but it had got tied up in the sword knot and he could not free it. Instead he grasped the standard, intending to use it as a weapon. However, glancing down at a man who had been shot, he noticed that he was a British soldier. He heard an officer exclaim crossly, "It's always the case, we always lose more men by our own people than we do by the enemy."

As the 52nd plodded on, it got caught in some crossfire and Leeke thought to himself how awful it would be if he was killed or wounded right at the end of the battle when the enemy was defeated. He also wondered what would become of his soul if he was killed. He comforted himself with the thought that those who believe in Jesus Christ would be saved. These morbid thoughts were put out of his head when the regiment halted close to the main chaussée to reorganize itself, for it was then that Wellington rode down and had a word with Colborne. Leeke turned round and distinctly heard

Wellington saying, "Well done, Colborne! Well done! Go on, don't give them time to rally."

Bullets had started to whizz round Leeke and he had a nasty feeling that the retreating French were aiming at him and the standard. Then he realized that they were probably aiming at the Commander-in-Chief. Lord Uxbridge certainly thought the Duke was in danger because he rode up saying, "For God's sake, Duke, don't expose yourself so, you know what a valuable life yours is." Wellington, who had led a charmed life all day, merely replied, "I'll be satisfied when I see those fellows go."

In fact it was poor Uxbridge who was wounded, not Wellington. Some grapeshot smashed into his knee, having passed over the neck of Wellington's horse on its course. It was said that while Wellington was watching the retreating French, Uxbridge exclaimed, "By God, Sir, I've lost my leg." Wellington removing his telescope observed, "By God Sir, so you have." Leeke did not see the incident because he was on the march again, this time in the front line. It occurred to him that if Napoleon was with the troops who were bringing up the rear of the French army, then Napoleon and Wellington were closer together than they had been during the battle, while he, Ensign Leeke, being right up in front, was the foremost man in the British army and the one nearest the French Emperor.

11

Nightfall

At Rossomme where Napoleon had had his headquarters for part of the day, the 52nd halted, piled up their arms in a pyramid so that they could pick them out easily, and camped for the night. The roll call of each company was called out by the sergeants, and Leeke noticed that in the case of absence, the men would say what had happened to the individual in question. The final reckoning was 38 killed and 168 wounded. The exhausted survivors laid themselves down on the ground to sleep barely aware that around them some 54,000 men and thousands of horses lay wounded, dying or dead on the cramped battlefield.

Leeke lay down too but he found that he was too tense to sleep. The edge had been taken off his hunger by a hunk of bread Rhodes had found in a French knapsack. He had offered some to Leeke with the words, "Won't you have a slice of bread, Mr Leeke? I am sure you deserve it, sir!" But he was deaf from cannon fire and terribly thirsty. He asked whether anyone could give him some water and was touched when four or five men thrust out their canteens towards him.

He joined his fellow officers round a blazing fire as an equal. He had survived his baptism of fire and no longer felt like a new boy. While they were discussing the events of the battle, cheering was heard in the direction from which they had come. An officer coming up told them that it came from those who had seen the meeting of Wellington and Blücher on the road between La Belle Alliance and Rossomme. The old Prussian hero had leant forward from his horse to kiss Wellington, exclaiming "Quelle affaire" in his bad French.

The Prussians had taken up the pursuit of the French. As they marched past the 52nd they played the British National Anthem to show their respect. One of their officers clasped the colour that Leeke was still holding and patted him on the back, saying, "Brave Anglais." Leeke took the opportunity of buying two horses from them at a very cheap price. The horses had been picked up from abandoned French guns. He did not really need the horses but he bought them because he did not like to see the Prussians walking off with everything. His fellow officers were delighted, not only because he presented one of the horses to them, but because a quart bottle of brandy was found on one of the saddles.

Leeke finally lay down on the ground head to head with another officer who had made himself a sort of straw shelter. His last thoughts before sleeping were of the dead and wounded soldiers of all nationalities who were lying out on the battlefield. The slaughter of the last ten hours had made a deep impression on the kind-hearted seventeen-year-old. Although he did not know it yet, the seeds of a different life, a life dedicated to God, had been sown in the depths of his being.

Christian and Louis Von Ompteda were camping out with the remnants of their uncle's battalion in the middle of the battlefield. They were not only tired and hungry but emotionally shattered. Someone had found their uncle's body by the garden hedge of La Haye Sainte late that evening. There was a single bullet hole in the collar of the coat. Every object of value such as his ring, seal and coins had been removed, but at least he had been left with his clothes. In order to prevent anything worse happening to the body the boys were watching over it.

All night long they were aware of the horrors on the battle-field. They could hear men crying out in delirium, shrieking in agony and begging for water. Nobody was doing anything to help them because it was dark and there were no medicines, spare blankets or even water. The wounded must wait until morning when they would be collected up by their regiments. The French would be attended to last of all. The boys could make out plunderers moving stealthily through the darkness.

What made the brothers sad was the thought that their uncle had died without seeing his homeland again. They knew how much he had hated living in exile and how much he had been looking forward to giving up his profession in the army so that he could live in quiet retirement in Hanover. He had not even lived long enough to see the French vanquished. When he had charged off to his death, he must have thought that the end for the Allies was very near. The boys talked about their own future, but did not feel that they could do what their uncle had wanted by leaving the army. They liked being soldiers and wanted to continue their military careers. And now they had the shining example of their uncle before them they wanted to maintain the high military standards he had laid down.

Back in Brussels, William Lennox retired to his comfort-able bed without knowing the outcome of the battle. He and his father had returned from the battlefield to find the capital seething with alarms. The hopes of the British residents had been raised by the arrival of thousands of French prisoners, only to be dashed again by the headlong flight of the Cumberland Hussars. People were scurrying about the streets, looking desperately for vehicles to take them out of Brussels. The wharf was crowded and the barges to Antwerp packed. The Richmonds had carriage horses ready, but Wellington had promised to send them word if they needed to flee and they did not intend to do so before hearing from him.

William found his sister Georgina busy preparing lint and extracting juice from cherries for use on the wounded. Lint, a soft cloth made from flax and cherry juice was thought to heal wounds. She had wasted the morning pacing up and down wringing her hands while the cannon growled in the distance like thunder. In the afternoon she had gone to the house of friends for news and had seen Lord Fitzroy Somerset and the Prince of Orange brought in wounded. Now she was keeping busy to distract her thoughts. Her lint and cherry water would be sorely needed by the good ladies who were attending the wounded in the streets.

Throughout the long evening visitors came to call, but none of them had definite news. The writer Thomas Creevey, who had been around and about a good deal, was full of interesting information. He told them that the locals were drinking in the cafés in the suburbs as if nothing was happening. Some were openly pro-French and he had heard that a banquet was being prepared for Napoleon. Although all the signs were bad, Creevey himself had not lost hope. He had noticed that wagons with supplies were still going towards the village of Waterloo from Brussels. This meant that orders were being sent from the front proving that the Allied army was not yet in ruins. William inclined to agree with Creevey. In addition, he had something that Creevey did not have, and that was infinite faith in Wellington.

When night fell and the French were in retreat, Mrs Adwicke gathered up Mary and the baby and went in search of John Adwicke. They picked their way along the road between fields littered with the dead and dying until they came to the spot where the 32nd had spent the day. There they found him wounded but alive. A musket ball had lodged in his right thigh some time during the afternoon. He had been dragged into the centre of the square where he had remained until the regiment dashed off the ridge in pursuit of the enemy.

John Adwicke was relieved to see his family because he was thirsty and in pain. Mrs Adwicke bound up his thigh and gave him something to eat and drink while other wounded soldiers looked on enviously. It was at times like these that it was an advantage to be married. Much restored by his wife's attention, John Adwicke managed to clamber to his feet, and by putting his weight on Mrs Adwicke he was able to hop and shuffle his way along, while Mary trotted alongside with the baby in her arms. They were fortunate to be so near to the crossroads and more fortunate still to come upon a cart with enough room for the wounded sergeant.

When they reached Brussels it was getting on for midnight. There were wounded soldiers lying in the streets because all six hospitals were full to overflowing. Mrs Adwicke wanted proper shelter so she set off to see what she could find. During her search she came across Mrs Deacon whom she had last seen looking for her husband on the night before the battle. This faithful woman had found him with nothing worse than a ball in his arm and she was now happily looking forward to the birth of her fourth child.

At last an empty space was found in the town hall and the Adwickes settled themselves down on the floor for what remained of the night. Nothing could be done for the wound until the surgeon saw it in the morning. Then he would have to face the risk of an operation and the likelihood of gangrene. But they would not think of that now. They were just grateful to be together and to be alive when the odds had been against it.

12

The Aftermath

Two days after the battle, William Lennox revisited the scene of the action, feeling very superior to Creevey and the others who were doing the same thing. After all, he had seen the start of the battle with his own eyes. As he rode down the chaussée there were signs of the recent fighting everywhere. Mounds of fresh earth marked the communal graves where heaps of dead bodies had been buried. Wounded Frenchmen were still lying around waiting for someone to help them. Some of the townsfolk were so shocked by the sight that they were bringing them back to Brussels in their coaches.

When he reached the village of Waterloo, Lennox was touched to find that the names of the officers that had been chalked up on the doors were still visible. He paused in front of the inn where Wellington had spent the night after the battle, and thought of the great man who was such a friend of his family. Those who had seen Wellington after the battle all told the same story. He had been in sombre mood, stricken by the terrible losses his army had sustained. He had dined in silence at the inn table that had been laid out for his staff. Only one other chair was taken, and each time the door opened Wellington looked up to see if one of his young officers had come in. He had drunk only one toast and that "to the memory of the Peninsular War." Then he had gone to bed on a pallet because Sir Alexander Gordon was dying in his bed.

He was awakened at three in the morning with the news of Gordon's death and a further list of casualties. As he listened to the roll call of names, tears of sorrow had coursed down his cheeks. "Well, thank God, I don't know what it is to lose a battle; but certainly nothing can be more painful than to gain one with the loss of so many of one's friends," he had said.

It was not only friends and officers that Wellington mourned, but also all the ordinary soldiers who had laid down their lives. He was determined to obtain a Waterloo medal for every private soldier who had fought in the battle. Neither did he boast of his victory. As he admitted to Creevey on his return to Brussels, "It has been a damned nice thing – the nearest run thing you ever saw in your life." Lennox was told that Sir William de Lancey was dying in a little cottage just outside the village. It seemed that there was nothing to be done. His new and adored young wife was with him, and according to her own wishes she was feeding and tending him by herself.

Lennox could not resist paying a call on Mr Paris in whose house Lord Uxbridge's leg had been amputated. The leg was already famous. Mr Paris, a Belgian with a shrewd business sense, had buried the leg in a coffin in the garden and was planning a plaque of commemoration to the leg of the illustrious and valiant cavalry commander. He was already charging people who wanted to see the boot that had been cut off the leg before the operation. Apparently Uxbridge's behaviour during the operation had been unbelievable. No word of agony had passed his lips. He had not even grasped a friendly hand as was the custom. His only complaint was to say that he thought the saw was not as sharp as it might have been. When it was all over, his pulse had not changed, and he was able to crack a joke. "I have been a beau these forty-seven years, and it would not be fair to cut the young men out any longer."

When Lennox reached the battlefield he was struck by the deathly silence in contrast to the sounds of battle he had heard before. The whole area was covered in objects that at first he mistook for crows. But a closer look showed them to be hats, cockades, letters, papers, bits of uniform, parts of harnesses and other bits of debris. The large armaments, cannon and the like, had been cleared off the field by the army, and all articles of value had long since been removed by scavengers. Some peasants were picking over the tattered objects that were left.

There were also more respectable citizens in search of souvenirs. Some of them were chipping bits from the elm tree that had served as Wellington's headquarters. It was obvious that if the tree was not cut down and removed to safety there would soon be nothing left of it.

Lennox rode along, first to the spot where he had stood during the exciting charge of the Union Brigade led by Major-General Sir William Ponsonby. He remembered how frightened he had been of his horse running away with him. He thought now of Pack who was injured, and Ponsonby and Picton, who were dead. The gallant Picton had been carried to the rear where it was discovered that he had been concealing a bad injury received at Quatre Bras, about which no one had known except his valet.

William thought of the amazing story that was doing the rounds about another Ponsonby who had had a miraculous escape. During the cavalry charge Lieutenant-Colonel Frederick Ponsonby of the 12th Light Dragoons was injured in both arms before receiving a sabre blow to the head that unhorsed him. On recovering his senses he raised his head to look around whereupon he was struck by a lance through his back. Bleeding from the mouth and helpless he was then robbed of three dollars by a French sharpshooter. Shortly afterwards a more friendly French officer gave him a swig of brandy and directed him to be laid on his side with a knapsack under his head. At the end of the battle he was tossed and turned on the ground by the hooves of Prussian cavalry in pursuit of the French. Even then his agony was not at an end because a dying Royal Dragoon fell on him pinning him down so that he could not move. Help came around midnight when an English soldier found him, released him from the dying Dragoon and stood guard over him until dawn.

Much moved by his memories, Lennox rode quickly on down to the cluster of farms which had guarded Wellington's left wing. The Dutch troops had done very well here. The farmhouses had changed hands several times during the day, but the troops had held their ground until the Prussians had arrived to assist them. This had not been until the evening, and then might not have happened at all but for one of those lucky moments that occurred in the battle. The Commander of the 1st Prussian Corps, thinking that the Allies were in retreat when he first came up, was not prepared to involve his soldiers until the rest of his army had arrived. He was therefore turning away when Von Müffling, noticed him and galloped up in the greatest agitation. He assured the Commander that the Allies were standing fast but that the battle was lost if the Prussians did not come back. They had taken so long to arrive on the battlefield, not because they had been intercepted by Grouchy, who never caught up with them, but because they had been dogged by difficulties coming across country from Wavre. But they had arrived in time to turn the tide against the French, and Wellington had been the first to express his gratitude.

Lennox returned along the ridge and took a detour down the road to inspect the farmhouse of La Haye Sainte. The buildings so valiantly defend by Major Baring and the KGL and then lost to the French, had been severely damaged by musket shot and fire. The crops in the field had been destroyed and the trees in the orchard hung in tatters. The sandpit opposite, where the 95th Rifles had stood for much of the day, was stained with blood. On the hillock behind was a communal grave where Colonel Von Ompteda and ten other officers had been buried.

To the right of the crossroads a party of Dutchmen were paying homage to the spot where the Prince of Orange had been wounded. Lennox, who knew the Prince well, was irritated by the way he was strutting around Brussels claiming the entire victory for himself and his troops. Prominent citizens in Brussels had already started to plan the erection of a huge monument on the historic spot.

Hougoumont was an even more devastating sight than La Haye Sainte. The château had been gutted by fire, and the stables and barns had been burnt to the ground. The courtyard was full of visitors because the defence of Hougoumont was already a legend. They were looking at the massive farm gates that had been closed in the nick of time. How triumphant Wellington had been when he turned to Müffling and said, "You see, Macdonnell has held Hougoumont." The visitors gazed down the well now stuffed with dead bodies, and gathered round the altar of the little chapel where the fire had miraculously stopped at the feet of the statue of Christ.

Van Cutsem, the Belgian gardener, was in his element, showing the sights to all comers. William, who spoke excellent French, had a conversation with him and learnt the sad story of the French drummer boy. He could well imagine the boy's terror when he had found himself alone, and his comrades dead around him. Van Cutsem did not know what had become of the boy. He might have died when the château caught fire, or he might have slipped out of the courtyard unnoticed when the French were in retreat.

From Hougoumont Lennox cut across country in the direction of La Belle Alliance. In the shattered woods to the south he came across more wounded Frenchmen who had not yet been collected. When he reached the ridge of La Belle Alliance he thought of the thousands and thousands of valiant French soldiers who had died fighting for their Emperor. A woman had been found among them. She had been dressed in the uniform of a cavalry officer and must have followed her lover to war. He passed the celebrated spot where Blücher and Wellington had met after the battle. Blücher had wanted to name the battle 'La Belle Alliance' but Wellington had followed his usual custom of naming his battle after his head-quarters of the night before, in this case Waterloo.

A little further on was the inn called Le Caillou. The innkeeper had been in the thick of the comings and goings for days and was still in a state of excitement. He had enter-tained British officers on their way to Quatre Bras on the sixteenth, and again in the retreat upon Waterloo on the seventeenth. Fast on their heels came Napoleon, who had done him the honour of sleeping there. And now he was having again to adapt himself to the victorious Allies.

On the way home Lennox thought about the two commanders and the different ways in which they had directed the battle. Napoleon had made the grave mistake of underrating his opponent. His tactics were uninspired. As Wellington, wrote to a friend after the battle. "Napoleon did not manoeuvre at all. He just moved forward in the old style in columns and was driven off in the old style." On the other hand, Wellington had been inspired by Napoleon to do his best. Somehow he had always appeared where he was most needed. He had risked his life throughout the day as he saw to vital details, plugged the gaps in his lines and rallied his soldiers. He had been neither boasting nor exaggerating when he told Creevey, "By God! I don't think it would have done if I had not been there."

13

Memories

The victory made Wellington very rich and very famous. He was to live for another thirty-seven years during which time he was to become Commander-in-Chief of the British Army, Prime Minister and a Field-Marshal in the armies of seven countries. He was presented with a country house at Stratfield Saye and Apsley House (now partly a museum) on Hyde Park corner in London became something of a national memorial. At home Wellington ate off hand-painted porcelain dinner services given to him by grateful nations. His eyes feasted on valuable pictures that were gifted to him by the Spanish. When he gave his annual dinner party for surviving officers on the 18 June the long table was decorated with huge silver centre pieces depicting his victories. Crowds always gathered in front of Apsley House on the eve of the dinner to watch the officers of Waterloo in their resplendent uniforms arriving at the front door.

The importance of Napoleon's defeat was instantly recognized around the world. Waterloo became a legend and a popular place name, Waterloo station in London being the most famous. Veterans began to be called 'Waterloo men.' The phrase 'to meet one's Waterloo' (meaning to be defeated) entered the English language. Statues and plaques to the fallen were erected all over Britain. A statue of Wellington mounted on a horse can be seen on the traffic island facing Apsley House. Even Wellington's valiant horse Copenhagen was not forgotten. When he finally died in 1836 a plaque in his honour was erected at Stratfield Saye.

After his humiliating defeat Napoleon tried to hang onto power but was overthrown by the allies and sent into exile on the island of St Helena where he died aged fifty-seven. Marshal Ney who had had five horses shot under him during the battle paid a heavier price. He was taken to the Luxembourg Gardens to face a firing squad of sixty veterans. There he showed the courage for which he was famed. Refusing a blindfold, he said, "Soldiers, when I give the command to fire, fire straight at the heart. Wait for the order, it will be my last to you." Prince Jerome Bonaparte who had been seen fleeing from Hougoumont in a carriage was allowed to continue his dissolute life until he died. Many of the French marshals took office under Louis XVIII, the restored king.

The battlefield itself and the village of Waterloo became a tourist attraction and remains so to this day. The little house where Uxbridge's leg had been sawn off has hardly changed. After the amputation the leg was buried in the garden but later reappeared under a glass case to be viewed by paying visitors. Much later a stone tomb inscribed to the leg of the illustrious Lord Uxbridge was erected in the garden and is still there though it does not in fact contain the leg. The most splendid monument of all was erected on the ridge of Mont St Jean where the Prince of Orange was wounded. It consists of a huge conical earth mound 43m high topped by a bronze lion on a plinth. It was commissioned by the Prince's father King William of the Netherlands and was completed in 1826.

THE LION MONUMENT

To fill the mound, much of the ridge had been leveled which led Wellington to declare when he visited years later, "They have altered my field of battle!" They have indeed but at the top of 226 steps it is possible to have a fine view of the rest of the battlefield.

Many survivors had missing limbs with which to remember the battle. Lieutenant-Colonel Frederick Ponsonby not only survived his mauling on the battlefield but an operation afterwards. He must have had the constitution of an ox because he became a Major-General and lived for another twenty-two years.

Even the ordinary soldiers were better rewarded than usual. Wounded men received pensions. Every soldier who was present could claim two years worth of extra pay and in 1816 they received a special Waterloo medal. This was the first time a medal had been given universally to all ranks alike and it was usually worn with immense pride. Some civilians showed their appreciation in practical ways. The rector of a church in Suffolk left a legacy of £500 in his will 'to the bravest man in England.' The choice fell upon Sir James Macdonnell for closing the gates at Hougoumont. Macdonnell declared that he was not alone in this and wanted to share the money with Corporal James Graham.

The victory became incorporated into various regimental symbols. Maitland's Ist Foot Guards were awarded the title of Grenadier Guards and adopted the bearskin headdress. The Household Cavalry started to wear the cuirasse as body armour. The Royal Dragoons who had captured the eagle of the 105th regiment assumed the eagle as its badge. It is now worn as an armband by the Blues and Royals (it's successor regiment). In recognition of the deadly effect of the French lance, the British cavalry began to use it as a weapon of choice. Although the 32nd Foot is now the Light Infantry and the 52nd Light Infantry is called the Royal Green Jackets, their valiant role at Waterloo is recorded in their regimental histories.

Memoirs, including one by de Lancey's heart-broken widow poured off the press. Military historians rushed their versions to the printers, among them one by William Siborne, whose enormous floor model of the battle can be seen in the National Army Museum in London. Artists who had not even seen the battle used their imaginations to depict dramatic scenes on canvas. Portraits of Wellington, Napoleon, Blücher and their generals could be purchased as prints by members of the public.

Lennox, Leeke and the Von Ompteda boys had been lucky to survive the Battle of Waterloo and they never forgot it. Long after peace had been restored to Europe they were to remember the events of that harrowing but glorious day. Lord William Lennox never recovered the use of his eye, but his arm mended and he was able to take up his military life again. A great many years later he wrote some memoirs about his three years as aide-de-camp to the Duke of Wellington. Although he had been so young at the time he clearly remembered how he had ridden out to the battlefield on the day of the battle and the day after.

William Leeke stayed with the army until he decided that after all, the religious life was for him and, became a clergyman. When he was over sixty he wrote a history of his old regiment in which he described the Battle of Waterloo in the minutest detail. When the KGL was disbanded, the Von Ompteda boys stayed in the British army. The memory of their uncle was passed on, and inspired one of Christian's own sons to edit the diaries and letters of his great-uncle. Mary Adwicke stayed with the army until her father was discharged four years later for 'length of service' with a Waterloo medal and a record of good conduct. Mary, who otherwise had so little in common with the others, must also have had her memories of the historic 18 June.

Lightning Source UK Ltd.
Milton Keynes UK
UKOW06f1109250615

254056UK00002B/35/P

9 780957 070714